The Amazing W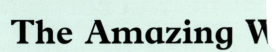

Contents

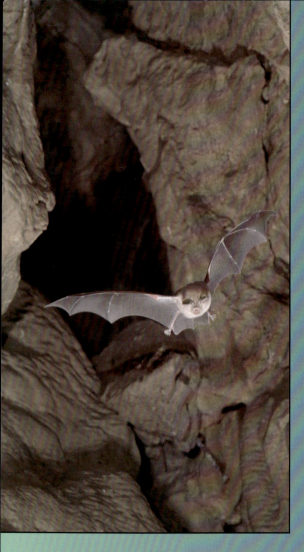

The Secret World of Caves

What do you think about when you hear the word *cave?* Deep, dark tunnels that twist and turn? Underground rivers? Millions of bats swooping overhead? Creatures without eyes or skin color? Ancient paintings? Homes for fierce predators, such as bears and bobcats?

Caves can be all of these things and more! Caves are natural openings in the earth and are found all over the world. Some caves are tiny, not even big enough to stand up in. Others are huge, with giant rooms and hundreds of miles of dark passageways winding deep beneath the surface of the earth.

A recent discovery in France shows a cave with drawings of ancient mammoths and rhinoceroses dating back more than 30,000 years! The cave is called Chauvet-Pont-d'Arc.

Some caves have amazing rock formations shaped like daggers, icicles, popcorn, or pearls. And most caves are loaded with life. They can have everything from shrimp without eyes to **bacteria** that give off poisonous gases. There are many different kinds of caves, from those that are carved by water flowing underground to those that are created by erupting volcanoes.

Stalactites

Stalagmites

Stalactites and **stalagmites** are cave formations that often look like icicles. They form as water either evaporates or slowly drips, leaving tiny deposits of a mineral behind. Stalactites hang from the ceiling, and stalagmites form from the ground up.

You can remember the difference because stalactites have a *c* for ceiling and stalagmites have a *g* for ground.

How Do Caves Form?

There are four things that can create a cave: rainfall, bacteria, waves from the sea, and **lava** from a volcano. Each of these cave makers creates a different type of cave, and each type of cave has certain characteristics that make it special.

Rainfall

Most of the world's caves are formed by something you drink every day: water. But caves aren't formed by the water from your tap. They are formed by rainfall.

As rain falls through the air, it picks up carbon dioxide, a gas that's naturally found in the air. When the rain hits the ground, it soaks into the soil and picks up more carbon dioxide. Rainwater that picks up carbon dioxide forms a very weak acid. This acid can dissolve a type of rock called limestone. When rainwater with carbon dioxide seeps into the cracks of limestone, it erodes the rock and creates caves.

7

Scientists have found bacteria living on the bottom of the ocean in thermal vents.

Extreme Bacteria

Some caves are created by the action of a stronger acid—an acid that forms from bacteria that live deep inside the earth. This might sound like a tale from a science fiction movie, but for years scientists have been learning about some amazing types of bacteria that can survive in places no other life has been found.

Yellowstone National Park

Scientists discovered some bacteria living in the hot springs of Yellowstone National Park at temperatures up to 170 degrees Fahrenheit. That's pretty hot for any living thing to survive. In the 1970s, scientists found bacteria living in thermal vents, which are springs of hot water on the bottom of the ocean. The bacteria were so deep that no sunlight could reach them.

Some bacteria create odd-looking formations. Some look like a runny nose and are called snottites.

Scientists call these bacteria **extremophiles** because they can live in harsh and extreme conditions. Scientists in the United States found some of these extreme bacteria living in caves. Some of the bacteria give off a gas that is poisonous to humans. The gas is carried by water into caves, where it mixes with oxygen and forms sulfuric acid. This acid is much stronger than the acid found in rainwater. It eats away at the limestone rock, leaving behind special formations.

Ocean Power

Some caves are formed by the powerful force of ocean waves. As these waves pound the base of cliffs along the sea, they can erode the weaker rocks at the bottom of the cliffs. Over time, the action of the waves, along with tides and heavy rain, can hollow out caves. Many creatures live in these sea caves, including crabs, sea stars, seals, and sea lions.

Sea lions

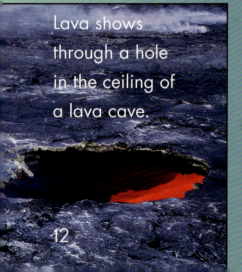

Lava shows through a hole in the ceiling of a lava cave.

Lava Caves

Some caves are formed from lava, which is molten rock from deep inside the earth that reaches the surface when a volcano erupts. But the lava doesn't erode rock. The cave actually forms in the middle of a lava flow.

When a volcano erupts, lava gushes out and flows down the sides of the volcano. The lava flows like a river, with the lava inside flowing faster than the lava on the sides.

The lava on the sides cools first, while the lava inside keeps flowing. This forms a hollow tube as the sides and top harden and the inside keeps flowing and eventually drains away.

These tubes or caves of lava can be huge, like a subway tunnel, or much smaller, like a drainpipe. One lava cave in Hawaii is more than 30 miles long!

A lava flow cools on the outside.

The hot lava inside drains away.

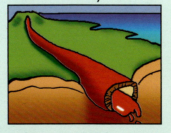

A long cave is formed.

Teeming with Life

You might think that living things could not survive in a cave since it's so dark and wet and cold. But caves are loaded with life—and not just bacteria. Scientists have studied hundreds of species of animals that spend all or part of their lives in caves. Each is especially adapted to survive in a habitat that would be a very hard place for humans to survive.

Entrance zone

Ferns grow in the entrance zone.

Cave Zones

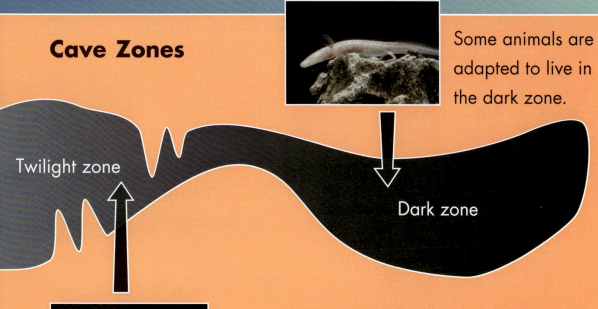

Twilight zone

Dark zone

Some animals are adapted to live in the dark zone.

A small amount of light reaches the twilight zone.

There are many different habitats in caves. The entrance zone is near the opening, where light can still enter. A little way in, it becomes darker in the twilight zone. The area where the light can no longer reach is called the dark zone. It's pitch black!

Vultures

Vulture eggs in a cave

Stopping By for a Visit

Some creatures and plants live near the entrance to a cave or right inside a cave opening, but you won't find them living deep inside where it's really dark. Mosses, ferns, and other moisture-loving plants that can't survive without sunlight often grow around the outside of a cave. Some birds, such as vultures, raise their chicks right inside since the cave helps protect them from harsh weather.

You might find snakes hiding out in caves on a hot summer day. That is because caves often stay cooler than the surrounding area. Other animals, such as bears, raccoons, and bobcats, will also use caves for dens, or places to hide out. Animals that use caves during part of the day or year but need to go outside for food are called cave guests.

Many types of bats live in caves, but bats can also live in trees, attics, and other dark places. Most cave-dwelling bats hunt outside at night. Some types of bats spend the winter in caves and migrate in summer, but others spend their whole lives in caves.

Living in the Dark

Some creatures that live in caves are especially adapted to life in the dark. They couldn't survive outside. Many creatures that spend their lives in the darkness of caves don't have eyes. Instead, they have special sensors that help them find food.

This blind crayfish lives its entire life in a cave. It does not need eyesight to survive in the darkness.

Some cave fish don't have eyes.

For example, many cave fish are blind. Some don't have eyes at all. Instead these fish have nerves on their heads and along their sides that sense tiny creatures in the water. Many of these fish are very small and live on very little food.

This tiny amphipod is colorless.

Part In, Part Out

Some animals spend time in caves, but they also live in other places. These animals include cave crickets, beetles, salamanders, snails, spiders, and worms. Many salamanders live in caves year-round because caves are moist and dark— a perfect habitat for them.

Cave crickets are often pale brown and have much smaller eyes than the crickets you see hopping around outside. Cave crickets live in warm, moist caves, but they sometimes leave the cave to find food.

Spider

Cave salamander

Cave crickets

Adapting to the Dark

Some insects and spiders have adapted to cave conditions. They are very dull in color and have longer legs and antennae. These adaptations help them walk through the mud and slime on the cave floor and feel their way in the dark.

Cave centipedes

Cave millipede

Cave cricket

21

Conserving Caves

For years, people have been exploring caves. Some of these explorers hope to discover new passageways and formations. Others are scientists who hope to dig up evidence of past human life or learn more about how caves form and what kinds of creatures live there. All of this exploration is helping us learn more about caves and find new species, medicines, and insights into our history. Exploration is also showing us that we need to do more to protect caves and their habitats from human threats, such as pollution and vandalism.

The study of caves is called speleology. People who explore caves are called spelunkers.

Luckily, people around the world are concerned about preserving caves, and many caves are now part of park systems and other protected areas. Many of the creatures in caves are protected too. There are also caving classes to help people learn how to explore caves safely without harming the formations and creatures that live there.

You can help preserve caves by learning about them and educating others. Caves are full of amazing secrets, and there's more to discover!

Glossary

bacteria: A type of life that can only be seen through a microscope. Bacteria live in plants, animals, soil, and water.

cave: An opening in the earth, which can form from running water, ocean waves, bacteria, and volcanic eruptions.

extremophiles: Bacteria and other microbes that can live in very harsh conditions.

lava: Molten rock that flows from a volcano or a large crack in the surface of the earth.

stalactites: Cave formations that look like icicles and hang from the ceiling.

stalagmites: Cave formations that look like upside-down icicles that form from the ground up.